© 2018 The Cycle

All Rights Reserved.

No part of this book may be reproduced, stored in a retrieval system, or transmitted by any means without the written permission of the author. The views expressed in this book are those of the authors and do not necessarily represent or reflect the views of this publishing company.

Published by Word Therapy Publishing, LLC

March 10, 2018

ISBN-13: 978-0975516348

ISBN-10: 0975516345

Printed in the United States of America all rights reserved under international copyright laws.

Cover Design by: Toni Henderson-Mayers

Word Therapy Publishing

P.O. Box 939

Hope Mills, NC 28348

www.wordtherapypublishing.com

Copyright page

ALL RRIGHTS RESERVED
All characters are fictional-
Amateurs wishing to arrange for this production of "The Cycle" must make application to Brian McClure Mayers at PO Box 939, Hope Mills, NC 28348 giving the following particulars:

(1) The name, town and theatre, hall, gym or any other building of the proposed
production.
(2) The maximum seating capacity of the theatre, hall, gym or any other building.
(3) Scale of tickets prices.
(4) The number of performances intended, and the dates thereof.

Upon receipt of these particulars performances through Brian McClure Mayers will quote terms and availability.
Stock royalty quotes on application to Brian McClure Mayers at PO Box 939, Hope Mills, NC 28348.
For all other rights than those stipulated above apply to Brian McClure Mayers at PO Box 939, Hope Mills, NC 28348.

Scripts and CD will be delivered two months prior to the production ONLY on receipt of the royalty quoted for all performances. No refunds once the scripts have been purchased. All fees mailed to Brian McClure Mayers at PO Box 939, Hope Mills, NC 28348 unless indicated otherwise.

Anyone presenting the play shall not commit or authorize any act or omission by which the copyright of the play or the right to copyright same may be impaired.

No changes shall be made in the play for the purpose of your production unless contacting Brian McClure Mayers.

The publication of this play does not imply that it is necessarily available for performance by amateurs or professionals. Amateurs and professionals considering a production are strongly advised in their own interests to apply to Brian McClure Mayers for consent before starting rehearsals, advertising, or booking a theatre, hall, gym or other buildings.

No part of this book may be reproduced, stored in a retrieval system, or transmitted in any form, by any means, including mechanical, electronic, photocopying, recording, videotaping, or otherwise, without the prior written permission of the publisher.

Music Use Note

Licensees are responsible for obtaining formal written permission from copyright owners to use copyrighted music in the performance of this play and are strongly cautioned to do so. If no such permission is obtained by the licensee, then licensee is solely responsible and liable for all music clearances and shall indemnify the copyright owners of the play and licensing of Brian McClure Mayers against any costs, expenses, losses and liabilities arising from the use of music by licensees.

IMPORTANT BILLING AND CREDIT REQUIREMENTS

All producer/producers of "The Cycle **must** *give credit to the Author of the Play in all programs distributed about performances of the play and in all instances in which the title of the Play appears for purposes of advertising, publicizing or otherwise exploiting the Play and/or a production. The name of the Author* **must** *also appear immediately following the title on the separate line, on which no other name appears. It* **must** *appear in size of type not less than 5 percent the size of the title type. Billing* **must** *be substantially as follows:*

THE CYCLE

by

Brian McClure Mayers

Originally Produced by Alphabet Theater Workshop

Toni Henderson-Mayers, Director

Performed at Fayetteville State University, Butler Theater

DEDICATION

Growing up in the inner city of Newark, New Jersey in the seventies had its challenges. Muggings, killings, riots, drugs and theft was high on the list of unlawful acts. One of the shameful acts that was over looked, was fatherless within the African American community and it's still prevalent today.

"The Cycle" is dedicated to all fathers who didn't have a positive relationship with their son. Our children are a gift from God. Fathers are responsible for providing, protecting and teaching their sons how to make good decisions. Being a father is a life time journey and part of it is to be the best father you can. Communication is key for all relationships, so I would like to say a few words to the men that played a pivotal role in my life.

Although my father wasn't a great communicator he did keep order in our house. It was my brothers that gave me those inspiring words, "You were born for a purpose," "Never give up on your goals" and "Hard work pays off along with dedication". So, I want to thank Edward,

Thaddeus and Richard Mayers for their words of wisdom and my upbringing.

To my grandfather Mr. Roy Washington Ellison. I still can remember his smile and strength. I have enjoyed all the summers I spent with him in North Carolina. I have seen him worked the fields and the farm. I have memories of him picking up the back of a 1957 Ford truck and moving it from the driveway to the back of the garage. We used to sit on the stairs and talk about my favorite cowboy while eating a butter pecan ice cream cone. You had a heart of gold and thank you sharing it with me. And finally thank you for all the nickels so I could buy those pickles.

To Malcolm Silvera better known as "Paco". I met him in my early thirties after recently getting married. Immediately I was drawn to his walk in the Lord and his understanding of scriptures from the bible. Paco shared his experience in his marriage and what it takes to sustain it. His true love for God is incredible and he is my hero. If I could just wear one of your shoes, then I would be half the man you are. Thank you Paco for all your teachings.

I am humbled that my Lord and Savior Jesus Christ allowed me to create this play and the opportunity to become a father to my sons Sean Brian Mayers and Christian McClure Mayers. I love you and thank you for being a blessing to me.

The Cycle is a riveting story of three generations of men and the challenges they face in the times they live. Their stories are both compelling and humorous. This play will educate, entertain and explain how curses are past down from generation to generation. These curses have slowly eaten away at the family, specifically, African American men. Laugh and cry with three of the most colorful characters that help paint a very graphic picture of life as they know it. Learn what has destroyed these men. Discover how these curses developed. Find new ways in your heart and through this play, on how to break, "*The Cycle*".

Running Time- 35 minutes

Performance Time- 57 minutes

CHARACTERS

PINK PICKLE PEN PETERSON III- Early sixties

SELEAK SELEEM ALI- MEAN ALI ARKBAK- Early forties

ROB- Early twenties

SPOKEN

"I might not be around for the next ten to twenty years, but before I go there something you need to know. It's time to break the cycle! It's time to break all the strong holds in your life, rather its drugs, bad relationship or being miss educated."

RAP SONG

It doesn't matter if you red white black or brown another frown on a child face cous he

moving from place to place starting out like a reckon ball knocking down a building

popping out of a story book playing that valiant fifteen and mean with know dream just a

matter of time for another crime scene now you twenty years old big and bold can't be

told and the story unfold about your dad that you wish you had swimming mad like a

trout big lip poked out knocked out another body count. Pops shoulda came home, pops

*never phoned or a letter woulda been better
but it doesn't matter cous the dead can't*

*speak no hugs from cheek to cheek
representing a man your weak no technique
you sneak*

*so don't blink! Like a flash from the pass
your son is gone no time spend you know*

*you'll wrong, but God gives second chances
so get with it commit it and break the cycle*

and walk like one of his disciples.

I'm talking about the cycle cycle

It's time to break the cycle cycle

What is your cycle cycle?

Here's another cycle cycle

ACT 1

Scene 1

SETTING:

Pictures of saloons, churches, and moonshine is shown on a projection screen. It's a breezy summer night and the stars are shimming over the moon in Columbia, South Carolina. Down center stage is an old wooden chair. Center stage right is an old wooden bench with a bible. Center Stage left a is bar, down center stage right is an outhouse w/sign with a large pot, and a broom handle. Down center stage left is a small table with empty liquor bottles.

AT RISE:

PINK PICKLEPEN PETERSON III enters talking to himself drinking liquor; music fades away.

PINK PICKLE PEN PETERSON III

I'm more tired than a hog waiting to be killed in a slaughter house. Back hurting, feet hurting, head hurting, but the main thing hurting is my stomach. Every now and then I get this pain in my stomach. This is a cruel world we are living in today. People can't get along, People playing the same old song. The boss man doesn't wanta pay you. Can't get my feet rubbed. I tried get a free drink, I wish…

Pink notices the audience.

Oh, I'm sorry! I didn't see you good folks sitting here tonight. Well allow me to introduce myself; my name is Pink Pickle Pen Peterson the III. I was born and raised in a shotgun house in South Carolina. It was me, my momma, my sister and my poppa and I'm the only one left here to tell this story. You see when I was a little fellow in South Carolina; I use to travel down the creek with Buba, Gop, and Letha Mae. We used to look at the water flow and make mud pies all day.

Stands up

Now Letha was my sister. She was four years older than me and she use to beat me up every single day, and that child had a mouth on her! Why Lethe ah sass anybody, didn't make no differ who it was, except mama. One day momma said Lethe go down yonder to the market, and Lethe said just a second. It only took a second for momma to hit her in the face with that iron skillet. Yes sir!

Takes a drink and feels pain in his stomach. I'll tell you mama didn't play. Momma stood bout six foot four two hunet and forty-five pounds, something like that. Momma was just as sweet as sugar cane growing by the corn field, and prettiest thang you ever wanta lay eyes on too! Her skin was like a coco brown, she looked like an oversize walnut when the moon hit her just right. Hair was just as fine as a horse's tail. She was seventy-five percent Cherokee. Momma could burn too; the best meal she cooked was "what you'll got", that means everything you got put it in a pot. Momma cooked for everybody in town especially the church. If you ever wanta to find my momma, all you have to do is go down at the end of the woods by the dirty swamp where the dead fishes at. There's a church down there
name Jesus Saves All Sinners.

Sits on bench

Reverence Jelly Back is the pastor there.
Momma was the mother of the church, the
cook, sung in the choir, on the mother board,
on the usher board, on the pastor aid board,
on the nurse's board, on the trustee board,
on the deaconess board and on the auxiliary.
Come think of it she was the board. Momma
use ta carried a thirty-eight on her hip and
she'd put a slug in you if you double cross
her. She shot at papa a few times for not
finding a job.

A moment to reflect
When my momma died, she died with a
bible in her hand her last words was
remember me in your kingdom. I thought
the kingdom was the church; mama spent so
much time there I thought that was where
heaven was. I miss you Mama, rest in
peace.

Takes a drink more pain in his stomach.
My momma died when I was ten years old
so that left my poppa in charge. Now poppa
was a different type of animal. I don't
member too much bout poppa. But poppa
stood bout five two a hunet and two pounds
something like that. poppa was a carpenter
by trade, well at lease he thought he was.
The only thing I saw poppa fix was a drink.

Walks to the outhouse and Fix a drink.

Poppa would be in the outhouse mixing it up! You could smell that corn liquor from here to kingdom come! poppa would cut up that corn and add that syrup, sugar and more sugar, yeast, herbs and God knows what else he added. My poppa taught me two things, how not to work and how to hold my liquor. The first-time poppa gave me some of that corn liquor I like to die, all I could say was put it out! Put it out! It felt like somebody struck a match to my black behind.

Pretend to strike a match on his behind. Yes sir! I'll tell you my throat was on fire. I thought it done burned a hole in my chest. I been drinking so long my chest don't even burn no more. Once poppa had that corn liquor in his blood
good Gugu Mugger. Poppa would tell you everything under the sun, how many women he kept company with, the last time he been to the moon and how he can keep from finding a job. We always knew when poppa had too much of a taste. Poppa's favorite words was boy, I'm going to beat you till your head croak like okra! Don't you ever tell a bold face lie to me! I going to beat you so bad that you ain't going to be able to sit on it for a month of Sundays! And give me another drink.

Takes a drink more pain in his stomach.
Walks center stage.

One day poppa found his way home, he was drunker then a skunk and poppa said Pink, hey Pink! I kept doing what I was doing. He said, boy didn't you hear me call your name Pink! I said no sir, I thought you was calling for a drink. Poppa was drinking so much you can smell that corn liquor coming out of his skin. But momma knew how to keep him in line. Momma would tell him get your black greases butt away from my table, you lazy good-for-nothing trifling bum! Poppa would get up.

Gets up and walks to the outhouse.

And take his little bitty self away from the table and go out to the outhouse and mixing it up. A few years later poppa died, papa died cuss his stomach was fill with this poison and he died in

his favorite place - in the outhouse. Well I don't miss him much, but I do miss drinking with poppa. I guess everybody gots to get a turn. Cheers to you poppa.

Takes a drink and sits, more pain in his stomach.

Now far as me, I've been drinking for the last fifty years and that's pretty much all I know. I went to the free client and the doctor told me Pink, if you take another drink you will surely die. Well, I'm still drinking and I'm still here to tell the story. So, let continue, I met Murolene in nineteen fifty-four. I put a baby in Murolene stomach in nineteen fifty-four. We gots married in nineteen fifty-four and I left her in nineteen fifty-four. Now it wasn't my fault the way we departed. Murolene found out that she had a baby in the oven so she wanted to get married, but I told her I told her, I'd not ready for those kinds of duties yet. Murolene told me I'd better gets ready and find a job. Now the only time I was put to work was when I had to do my chores for momma. Other than that, I haven't worked for the last fifty years, you see I'm on the borderline of being a bum and a wanderer, in fact I been wandering around all my life. So, one day Murolene said Pink, Pink get up! And I said I don't feel like getting up woman, and she said get your butt up you lazy no good nigger!

Stands up

And I said what did you call me? She said, I called you a lazy no good nigger! I said well at least I'm not a no count nigger! Because those kinds of niggers don't even count, yes

sir! I just packed my two pieces of clothes and left. I didn't even have time to see my baby being born and I really don't care. As I was walking out the door Murolene look me square in the eye and said, be careful of the toes you step on today, they might be connected to the foot that lead to the butt that you got to kiss tomorrow. You think that I'm lazy and trifling, don't you? But that's not true. I just enjoy doing nothing. I can't recall when the last time I took a bath. I tried to go down to
the office to get some social securities but they told me I don't have any monies in my account because I haven't worked anywhere. Do any of yawl have any money cause all I got left is a swig and I need my liquor to survive in this world. I'll take anything strong, gin, rum, brandy, white label blue label, black label but I really like the man with the stick, Johnny Walker Red… Well, getting back to Murolene. She started to grow on me like bacteria and I got enough of that. It's not that she was a bad woman or hard to look at. From the side, she was built like an old washing machine. You know the kind with the rollers. Murolene always told me I'm going straight to Hell with gasoline pants on, I said that will suit me well, as long as I can get me a drink when I get down there. I found out the baby she had

was a boy, and after twenty something years I finally got a chance to meet him. He came down from that big city, New York City; he had one of those big hats on in the middle of July. I know he must have been hotter than Hades. So, I said what might your name be boy? He said Selleck Saleem Ali- mean Ali Ark bar, but everybody calls me daddy. I told him I'm your daddy. He asks me why did I leave his momma. I said we didn't have the same ideas. He said why did you leave me? I said I knew I would have to work and I didn't feel like working. He said you no good lazy nigger! And I said well it's better than being a no count nigger! Because those kinds of nigger don't count. My son said he never want to see me again and he went back to New York City. I don't feel bad about not being there for my son, the only thing I could have taught him was how not to work and how to hold his liquor.

> *Takes his last drink and the pain in his stomach is unbearable.*

So, I thank you good folks for listening to my problems, I going to try to get a free drink before the shop close, and if yawl not here when I come back remember to always give yourself a drink.

> *Pink dies on stage and exits, music plays.*

SPOKEN

"Education, we live in a society where you have to be educated! Rather through some kind of training, learning a trade, or even going back to school. I prefer going back to school."

RAP SONG

What about the nerd that you heard that you shoulda hung with you and the crew with little boy blue doing the boogaloo as the class clown, let me break it down, so you want to be a jokester, a prankster wanta be gangster Al Capone is dead and gone gone gone now follow along. You go to school to learn to earn but you made a U-turn and now you concern so you return but you still unlearn and you living from day to day it was our ancestors who paved the way digging and crawling and scratching underground, listen to the sound of the bloodhounds after you and me 1865 we were set free to rebuild the family tree and there's a need to lead so let's start to feed the new breed another child is born, here comes the storm.

I'm talking about the cycle, cycle

It's time to break to the cycle, cycle

What is your cycle, cycle?

Here's another cycle, cycle

ACT 1

Scene 2

SETTING:

It's a cool night in New York on Hunts Points. Down stage left is a light pole that says "Hunts Point". Down center stage is a small table, belt, pills and needles. Center stage, right and left are bags of old clothes, pills, garbage and other debris. Music fades.

AT RISE:

Selleck Saleem Ali-mean Ali-Ark bar enter swaging and staggering from side to side.

SLEAK SELEEM ALI-MEAN ALI-ARKBAR

What's happening baby, right on my brothers and sisters, slip me some skin my friend and give me five on the black hand side, how yawl feel tonight? Solid! Allow me to introduce myself my name is Selleck Saleem Ali- mean Ali- Ark bar and no I'm not a Muslim I just like that way that sound baby but the people on the streets call me daddy. Now you just heard my old man Pink Pickle Pen Peterson the third tell his side of the story now I'm going to lay my side of the story on you, but before I get started I'm must tell you I'm feeling good up in here, I'm glad yawl was able to join me in the crack house tonight and I'm high as a kite, and man I love getting high. There no better feeling in the world, it's like you really really floating on a cloud that you can't come off. Its heavy baby I'm telling you its heavy. I'm not talking about this refer type of high,
I'm not talking about that drunk kind of high, I'm not even talking about popping pills and catching thrills kind of high, I'm talking about that kind of high that freezes the brain, that pure white cocaine.

Sits down

Yeah baby, so if you see me nodding in and out or falling asleep

> *Quickly falls asleep and wakes up.*

that's because I'm feeling super good. I feel so good up in here. I feel like running butt naked down the street but I don't want to frighten nobody. Now I know what you thinking, that I ani't nothing but a drug addict, and you right but it's not my fault the way I turned out. You are looking at a cat that is the product of the environment I grew up in. I grew up in the big apple baby where you had to hold your own just like papa was a rolling stone. Everything I learned I learned from my step dad and on the streets.

Fantasying

It all started when I was ten years old. We used to play a game call hot peas and butter, man I was the best that ever played the game. My friend cool breeze used to hide the belt and all the other girls and boys use to try to find the belt. Cool breeze would always wink his eye and tell me where the belt was. He would say you cold, you warm, you're hot, you are burning up! I always found the belt.

Stands up and grab the belt off the table and beat the seat of the chair.

And once I found that belt, I would set their butt on fire. I only caught the girls. I like beating girls. I would beat them girls like they stole something and send them home crying to their momma. Today things haven't changed one bit, but now I beat girls and women. When I send my ugly ladies out, you know they better have my money, because if they don't have my money I'll beat them like when I was little. That's right I said it; I take them eighteen to eighty cripple, blind and crazy.

Sit back down
You see I wasn't born with a silver spoon in my mouth, I been on my own since I was thirteen, my step dad convinced me that I could make more money on the streets than working a job and going to school, so at fourteen I drop out. By the time I was sixteen I was pimping women and driving a nineteen seventy-five Eldorado, and this El dog was macked out. It was pink and white with a fish tail flipping in the back. It had white wall tires and electric sun roof to match. A long CB antenna saying breaker breaker "119 I copy you good buddy" and the headlights look like a lady bug, the inside was laid out.

Nodding out

It had raccoon seat covers, electric seats that moved back and forward, tilted steering wheel with cruise control, AM, FM radio with an eight-track tape system playing Earth Wind and Fire that will blow your mind,

Take a sniff of cocaine

Man, this cocaine is right on time! Hot diggerdy dog! I used to pick up Scary Harry from the shooting gallery on and we would meet Joe Clip with the big lip and his brother Stan the man with the little hand. We all would pile up and eat murder burgers and get high all night. Now a lot times we got stopped by the fuzz, but they never thought about putting us in the slammer because we always gave them some of that Mr. Feel good, that pure cocaine baby! There were a lot of things the fuzz didn't care about, and one of them was domestic violence. My mother got knocked upside the head all the time. My mother tried to call the fuzz either they came too late or they didn't come at all. I thought every man suppose to beat on their women. Every time my step dad came home my mother better have his dinner on the table. If my mother didn't have his dinner on the table, he would take her in the back room and beat her real good, and that's how I'm feeling right now baby real good.

Stiff more cocaine

My mother was always either in the hospital, or the dentist office. Although my step dad enjoyed beating up my mother my step dad's thing was running numbers and selling nickel and dime bags. And you already know my angle getting high and pimping women.

Day dreaming

I once had a girl name Belinda she had a body that I always will remember. From the back, she was stack like a horse she had a lot of junk in the trunk, but when she turned around she looked like a bad car wreck. Belinda was the best street walker I ever had; she only short changed me once but that was one too many. After I broke her jaw in three places, Belinda never short changed me again. Sometimes I beat my street walkers just because I'm high or in a bad mood,

but I had to fire Belinda because she said I got her pregnant. She lied about that, because most of time all I saw was the back of her head any way. Well, come to find out the fool was pregnant and the only reason why she got pregnant is because she stopped taking the pill, and I don't use no saddle any way because I only go bare back riding.

Four years later Belinda came to one of my corners, my corner! And said here's your son. I told her you better get that nappy headed boy out of my face women before I smack you around like I use to do, and then that rock head boy started crying. He says daddy don't you love me? I said boy I don't even love myself, now you and your mama get out of my face you are blowing my high.

Takes a sniff of cocaine and gets up
Several years later I saw that same boy who grew up to be a man. He came to my crack house, he said do you remember me. I said no, he said I am your son you don't love me dad? I said man I don't even love myself. Before I could look up my son smacked me in the mouth. I tried to run but he caught me, then he started smacking me around the same way I use to smack his mother. Now I started. I started to hit back, but I was used to beaten women not men. My son lumped me up so bad, I thought I had two faces. I started looking like the elephant man, Finally, three months later I could talk to him.

Sits down

He asks me why I never claimed him as a son. I told him you are just one of many sons that I have, you just happen to show up. My son pulled out pistol and put it to my head and he said I don't have to kill you, you already dead; you're just walking around like the average crack head.

Rolls up his sleeve and tie a belt around his arm, start to feel bad about himself.
I really don't care about not being there for my son the only thing I could have taught him is how to get high and beat up women. Do you know what the biggest lie is? Getting high on your supply. Man, I've been getting high for the last thirty plus years and I not dead yet. If I have to I'll take that needle and bang it in my arms, and if I can't find a vein there I'll bang it in my hands until they become big as catcher's mitts or in my feet until they look like balloons filled with water, and if I can't get a vein in any of those places I'll bang it in my neck.

Put the needle in his neck.
Ah Yeah that feels so good! That's almost the perfect high. One thing about cocaine it goes straight to the brain and this can relief any pain. But I tell yawl I'm still trying to

get that first high, I wonder if I'll ever get it before I die…

Seleak dies on stage and exits, music play.

SPOKEN

"Most of the time a cycle starts with our parents, and our parents seen their parents cycle, and their parents seen their parents cycle."

RAP SONG

Born from a generation curse I seen worst beaten up till you black and blue, cuss you shoe black, fighting back like a trooper without a flaw its twenty to one a win is a win and now I'm sitting in the bull pin. Thinking about how it all started, 24-7 standing on the corner like you on Broadway getting paid sets the stage perhaps every day selling that crap that leaves your veins critical its only mental to stay afloat we came off the boat let's start to vote there always hope in GOD! Always seems to amaze me some people think that I'm crazy time and time again join and be his friend he with you till the end he coming back again flowing with the favor, Jesus the true savoir! Born from a generation curse, it doesn't matter if you're red white black or brown, born shoulda hung with born from a generation curse...

I'm talking about the cycle, cycle

It's time to break your cycle, cycle

So what is your cycle, cycle?

Yo listen up! It's time to break the cycle!

ACT 1

Scene 3

SETTING:

It's Friday morning at Trenton State Correction Facility. Down center stage is a small bed with a sign that reads "Lifers". Down center stage left is a tomb stone. Down center stage right is a bench with a sign that says "Death Row".

AT Rise:

Rob enters full of energy and ready to take on the world.

ROB

What's going on! Yo, Yo, my man what up! Yawl chilling or what? What's up black in the back? What's popping baby? It's going down tonight! Oh, it's on like popcorn, I'm at home now. I'm with my boys. Yeah let's get this party started. Now it's time for me to spread the gospel, I'm about to blow this roof off the building! You know what I'm saying? Yeah you heard the story of my dope head dad, how he was a wanted be a pimp daddy. After I beat my dad down I let him speak, so I said you remember me? I know you remember me? He says no, I said you the same nigger abandon me, but that's okay because I was born to keep it real, so let's push this story along. My slave name is Rob, but my boys call me steel. There's no doubt my mom and my boys gave me the right name, because robbing and stealing is what I do for a living. Yawl feel me? I'll rob your mother if she has enough money. All come on now I know I'm not the only one in here that robbed somebody before otherwise we wouldn't be sitting in the same jail cell. Man, I've been strong arming people since I was twelve years old, with a gun, a knife, chain, and my fist, so when see me walking the streets you at your own risk, and I'm the best at what I do, believe that! I come from the hard knocks streets of Newark, New Jersey where the rats are big as cats, where homelessness is a way of life, I'll rob you morning, noon, and night. See I'm the joker you better fear.

Sits.

Since my dad was never around, and my moms was nothing but a night hawk. I was always home by myself. Sometimes my moms wouldn't come home for weeks she was nothing but a freak that's when I decided to creep. I started sticking up kids for their bikes and reselling them for a higher price. At fifteen I was beaten people for their credit cards, while jacking cars in broad day light, but I would only jack the good cars like the Jags the Mercedes, beamers, porches. I would hit mainly the doctors and lawyer's offices.

Stands up.

And soon as they open their car door I'll sneak up behind them real slow then bum rush the show and said dig, give it up, Give it up nigger! You know what time it is! Most of them would pee in
their pants. I'll take the keys do a couple of donuts and I was out, there was no doubt I had all the clout. After I took the stereo speakers and anything else that was valuable, I would take it to my boys at the

chop shop and let them deal with it. It
wasn't long before that got old, so I finally
found my niche; I was attractive to B and
E's so I started breaking into people
households, but I didn't break into the
average home, so I started to roam to the
suburbs when all the monies at, those fools
always left the house keys under the door
mat. It didn't make a difference if they were
home or not, because I was determined to
get paid, I didn't care about a blockade and I
was never afraid regardless what was the
cost, because when I roll, I roll hard and I
never left a home empty handed. Listen up; I
got so good I was even robbing the blind
and little midgets with receding hairlines.
For three years, I was handling my business!
I was killing them! It all ended at seven
A.M, in the morning now that's only
because I miss read the signs of the truth,
soon I'll be walking in a jump suit. As I
walked in the court room with my P.D, there
I stood in my home boy stance, knowing
that I had a chance to hang out with my boys
again. When it was time for me to go in
front of the judge I stared at him straight
into his face, never realizing that I was in his
place. Before I knew it, the judge was
trying to send me up the river, hoping that I
would shiver and quiver, and when he said
twenty-five years, I knew who the lawgiver,

out of the twenty-five, I did twelve, and it was a rough twelve and all of them weren't pleasant. It all starts

with the process baby. You see everything is new when you enter the process. Yo check this out, I was thrown into the car with no rights read, beating in the head but I was never scared of a new home that how it's going to be, but there's one guarantee that I have a new addressee. I told them my name time after time while officers taking pictures for nightline. I was chain up! Strapped up! Buckled up! and now that I told you, being pushed along like march of the wooden soldiers. One by one they all peeked from the cage throwing up gang signs full of rage and when one kid came in not ready to die, he laid there motionless with a pencil in his eye. Fingerprints tells your whole life story, I had to submit because I was in a new territory. And, spades is a popular game and everything else remains the same, while slowly the numbers replace your name and some COs never takes the blame. I was walking through the cell while the fellows playing chess, I begin to realize that it's all a part of the process. One of the cages hold up to fifty people in the day room, jokers playing the tough role, but I ain't nobody bridegroom. I see it all baby. I trying to tell you I seen it all! Strip butt naked bare skin and all, time to line up! It's row call. Ringing out numbers from different places light faces hidden in dark spaces hung with their own shoelaces. Here comes the COs carrying their hardware by their side yelling who committed this homicide or was it suicide. Night of the living dead heads awake at dawn taunting the shy and quite ones who don't belong, putting food in their hair and setting their feet on fire while others sit and admire these vicious vampires. Clicked up like a pack of rats, while the gang leader is laid back, why he's just a scaredy cat. There is a place where no man wants to go, step into the hole with only your soul in creeps the cold feeling like the North Pole. Fifteen days ah past you by the system is designed to keep you color blind while your love ones continue to cry trying to figure out why? Kill another man with a switch blade laying in a pool of blood too late for first aid, slice and dice swinging his dreadlocks ready to be served for the wooden box. And slam bang goes the sound of a jail cell! Another body laying by the stairwell. Now I'm coming at yawl and I'm hitting you hard while passing the shank through the court yard. In the process, you have make your own bed while others getting jacked for their footwear.

Things happen in a blink of an eye while snitchers become a la la bye. Even convicts have to protect your rep because it's all about the process.

Sits.

While I was pulling time, I meet this girl name May, she saw through me right away. She said Steel oh Steel I can see you up to know good. I said I'm not the bad guy so consider me Robin Hood, I steal from the rich and give to the poor I'm the type of joker you can't I ignore. At first May choose to be rude, treating the brother like the average dude. I told her I'm up to do a quarter of a century just give the brother a chance, she said we unevenly yolk therefore it won't be no romance. I said I know the type that's when I decided to write. May said I'll tell you what I'll do, I'll pray for you and maybe one day I can be you're boo, I said cool so I had to go old school without breaking any rules. While I was in the process my roommate name was Doc. He was tall and dreary looking like a warlock, now I was shock he been around the block. Doc did a triple murder doing sixty years to life and one of his victims was his wife and I thought I was a low life. Doc had the look of death on his face while cuts and scares come from the boulevard trying to be a superstar.

He had tattoos from the top of his head to the tip of his shoe and each tattoo showed what he been though. His voice was rough and tough, old and gray from smoking so many years he

changed the atmosphere of all the tiers including the queers. Doc's hair was thin and fine, although he was approaching sixty-nine his brain was like an Einstein. We had long talks from the military to the sanctuary why we even talked about Tom and Jerry, but his favorite place was the library.
Doc taught me right from wrong along with the gospel songs, he told me how a man went down into the ground and three days later he rose with a crown. Doc slogan was knowledge is like a wildflower, and seeking wisdom comes from a higher power. It was like he poured all his tears in a cup, I drank it all until I was bellied up. As Doc got older his voice started to switch to another gear while the sound of his footsteps started to disappear.

Reflecting

Doc's words were like medicine to my bones. I can still hear the moans and groans of full blown aids that he once owned, and I still remember his tombstone. Doc had finally faded away like the ghost from Christmas past and all the other inmates paid their respect along with the staff. I realize I didn't see it all, I have so much to learn, I haven't even lived yet. Doc was a man, Doc was a good man! Yeah, he had his cycle just like anybody else. I only knew Doc for five years, but he poured fifty years of himself in to my soul. I miss man, I wish you was here with me. Why did you have to leave me here by myself, Doc was a father figure to me!

Emotional

He told me when you speak the word be bold and remember who's in control. Doc said Robert; he always called me Robert, never focus on what happen in the past, because you will be stuck in the past, focus on the present so you can look forward to a bright future. I never knew what Doc was talking about until I got out of the jail. One of the things I learned real fast was to respect the freedom that I have because when you are doing time you have no freedom. I can't afford to go back into the process.

Toward the audience

So, the question remains what is the cycle in your life? Is it the drugs that keep you plugged or you trying to be a thug? So, put down the guns and teach your daughters and sons that life is fun before you twenty-one. Everybody have different cycles in their life, one of the cycles our young people are face with is joining gangs that was something I could not be a part of. Why
would I want to join the Bloods, I don't want to come home bloody, or why would I would I want to join the Crips I most definitely don't would to come home cripple. School was another cycle I couldn't get with, but when I tried to read a job application I couldn't understand it. One thing about education it will open your mind, and yes earning a degree will take some time. So, let me give you one key to set you free, that it was Jesus Christ who delivered me.

NOTE: (Optional, Free by Darwin Hobbs)

(Optional if Rob want to sing the first verse)

BLACK OUT

THE SONG THE CYCLE

I might not be around for the next ten to twenty years, but before I go there something you need to know. It's time to break the cycle! It's time to break all the strong holds in your life, rather its drugs, bad relationship or being miss educated.

It doesn't matter if you red white black or brown another frown on a child face cuss

he moving from place to place starting out like a reckon ball knocking down a building

popping out of a story book playing that valiant fifteen and mean with know dream just a

matter of time for another crime scene now you twenty years old big and bold can't be

told and the story unfold about your dad that you wish you had swimming mad like a

trout big lip poked out knocked out another body count. Pops shoulda came home, pops

never phoned or a letter woulda been better but it doesn't matter cuss the dead can't

speak no hugs from cheek to cheek
representing a man your weak no technique
you sneak

so, don't blink! Like a flash from the pass
your son is gone no time spend you know

you'll wrong, but God gives second chances
so get with it commit it and break the cycle

and walk like one of his disciples.

I'm talking about the cycle cycle

It's time to break the cycle cycle

What is your cycle cycle?

Here's another cycle cycle

Education, we live in a society where you have to be educated! Rather through some kind of training, learning a trade, or even going back to school. I prefer going back to school.

What about the nerd that you heard that you shoulda hung with you and the crew with little

boy blue doing the boogaloo as the class
clown, let me break it down, so you want to

be a jokester, a prankster wanta be gangster
Al Capone is dead and gone now

follow along. You go to school to learn to
earn but you made a U-turn and now you

concern so you return but you still unlearn
and you living from day to day it was our

ancestors who paved the way digging and
crawling and scratching underground listen
to

the sound of the bloodhounds after you and
me 1865 we were set free to rebuild the

family tree and there's a need to lead so let's
start to feed the new breed another child is

born, here comes the storm.

I'm talking about the cycle, cycle

It's time to break to the cycle, cycle

What is your cycle, cycle?

Here's another cycle, cycle

Most of the time a cycle starts with our parents, and our parents seen their parents cycle, and their parents seen their parents cycle.

Born from a generation curse I seen worst beaten up till you black and blue, cuss you

shoe black, fighting back like a trooper without a flaw its twenty to one a win is a win

and now I'm sitting in the bull pen thinking about how it all started, 24-7 standing on the

corner like you on Broadway getting paid sets the stage perhaps even laid selling that

crap that leaves your veins critical its only mental to stay afloat we came off the boat lets

start to vote there always hope in GOD! Always seems to amaze me some people think

that I'm crazy time and time again join and be his friend he with you till the end he

coming back again flowing with the favor,
Jesus the true savoir!

Born from a generation curse, it doesn't matter if you're red white black or brown, born

from a generation curse, what about the nerd that you heard that you shoulda hung with,

born from a generation curse…

I'm talking about the cycle, cycle

It's time to break your cycle, cycle

So what is your cycle, cycle?

Yo- Yo my man, it's time to break the cycle!

Furniture

Scene One

Wooden chair
Wooden bench
Bible
Bar
Sign that reads Outhouse
Table
Empty liquor bottles

Scene Two

Two wooden chairs
Small table
Needles
Baking soda
Pills
Spoons
Rubbing alcohol
Belt
Bags of clothes
Empty garbage cans
Light pole that reads Hunts Point

Scene Three

Small bed
Bench
Pillow
Cover
Bar bells
Crate that read "The Hole"
Tomb Stone
Small table
Handcuffs
Picture of May

Props

Pink Pickle Pen Peterson III

Liquor bottle
Broom handle
Large pot
Knife
Ear of corn
Sugar
Yeast
Herbs
Syrup

Sleek Saleem Ali-Mean Ali-Ark bark

Cocaine
Needles
Baking soda
Pills
Spoons
Rubbing alcohol
Belt

Rob

Bible

Costumes

Pink Pickle Pen Peterson III

Fishermen hat
Dirty under shirt
Dirty overall pants
Slippers

Sleek Saleem Ali-Mean Ali-Ark bark

Pimp hat
Butterfly collar shirt
Bell bottom pants
Platform shoes

Four gold chains

Rob

Orange jail suit
Duo rag
Slippers

Language

Shot Gun House- A small narrow house.

Yonder- A distance from your current location.

Jelly Back- A scary person.

Slug- Bullet

Gugu Mugger- When a person feels good about themselves.

Croak Like Okra- Putting lumps on a person's head.

Bold Face Lie- Telling a lie with a straight face.

Boogaloo- A Silly type of dance.

Big Apple- New York City.

Silver Spoon- A person with a lot of money.

CB- A public two- way personal radio service.

Fuzz- Police Officer.

Junk in the Trunk- A big back-side.

Gospel- Truth.

Jacking- Taking someone personal possession.

Donuts- Doing burn outs by a vehicle.

B and E's- Robbing somebody house.

CO's- Correction Officer.

Boo- Friend or significant other.

Pink Pickle Pen Peterson III thinking about his wife Murolene.

Pink Pickle Pen Peterson III Sharing his mother cooking recipes.

Pink Pickle Pen Peterson III communicating with his mother from heaven.

Pink Pickle Pen Peterson III explain how his father use to beat him.

Pink Pickle Pen Peterson III boasting about how much liquor he can drink.

Pink Pickle Pen Peterson III Thinking about his son.

Selleck Saleem Ali-mean Ali-Ark bar makes himself at home.

Selleck Saleem Ali-mean Ali-Ark bar feeling good.

Selleck Saleem Ali-mean Ali-Ark bar when drugs start to affect his speech.

Selleck Saleem Ali-mean Ali-Ark bar after being beaten by his son.

Selleck Saleem Ali-mean Ali-Ark bar bragging about his girlfriend.

Selleck Saleem Ali-mean Ali-Ark bar last dose.

Rob first day in jail.

Rob explains where he's from.

Rob describes being in the hole.

Rob realizes he might never get out of jail.

Rob making the adjustment in jail.

Rob just found out his hero died.

Actor/Playwright Brian McClure Mayers

and

Director Toni Henderson-Mayers

What People are saying

Brian Mayers' book is a lesson in humanity--both what to do and what NOT to do. He addresses issues still pertinent to modern behavior while looking at the past as a driving force behind that behavior. It is a must-read and must-see piece of drama for any student of humankind.

Phoebe Hall, Professor
Performing and Fine Arts Department
Fayetteville State University

www.wordtherapypublishing.com

"A Message That Heals"

www.ingramcontent.com/pod-product-compliance
Lightning Source LLC
Chambersburg PA
CBHW071240090426
42736CB00014B/3158

THE ANTHROPOSOPHICAL WORLD SOCIETY